A First Book of
Dvořák

FOR THE BEGINNING PIANIST with DOWNLOADABLE MP3s

David Dutkanicz

Dover Publications, Inc.
Mineola, New York

All music available as downloadable MP3s!

Go to www.doverpublications.com/0486828905
to access these files.

Bibliographical Note

A First Book of Dvořák is a new work, first published by Dover Publications, Inc. in 2018.

International Standard Book Number

ISBN-13: 978-0-486-82890-9
ISBN-10: 0-486-82890-5

Manufactured in the United States by LSC Communications
82890501   2018
www.doverpublications.com

Contents

Author's Note

A First Book of Dvořák continues the tradition of making the world's greatest music accessible to all and is a welcome addition to Dover Publications' beginner piano library. A wide variety of Czech composer Antonín Dvořák's (1841–1904) works are presented here, highlighting his famous as well as lesser-known compositions.

There are two catalog numbers used. The standard opus (Op.), which is designated for works that were officially published and available to the public, are assigned in chronological order based on date of publication. The other cataloging number is the Burghauser (B.). This is in reference to the Czech musicologist Jarmil Michael Burghauser (1921–1997), who cataloged unpublished works and listed them by date of composition rather than publication. If you research any music, these numbers help to save time and ensure accuracy.

Phrasing and pedaling have been kept to a minimum so as to make the music less daunting. These can be filled in as progress is made. Fingerings also have been provided but should not be considered an absolute. Feel free to customize them to your own hands. The works are arranged according to approximate level of difficulty.

As a bonus, all the music in this book is available as downloadable MP3s at www.doverpublications.com/0486828905. Enjoy!

Pastorale *from* Czech Suite Op. 39

A *pastorale* is a musical composition intended to evoke images of nature and the countryside. This rustic melody is supported by a static left hand playing an open fifth (C–G). The effect is known as a *drone* and is reminiscent of old folk instruments.

Kyrie *from* Mass Op. 86

The *Kyrie* is the traditional first movement of the Mass. Dvořák composed this work in 1887 for the consecration of a private chapel. Note how the melody is repeated by the left hand in measure 5. This is known as *imitation*.

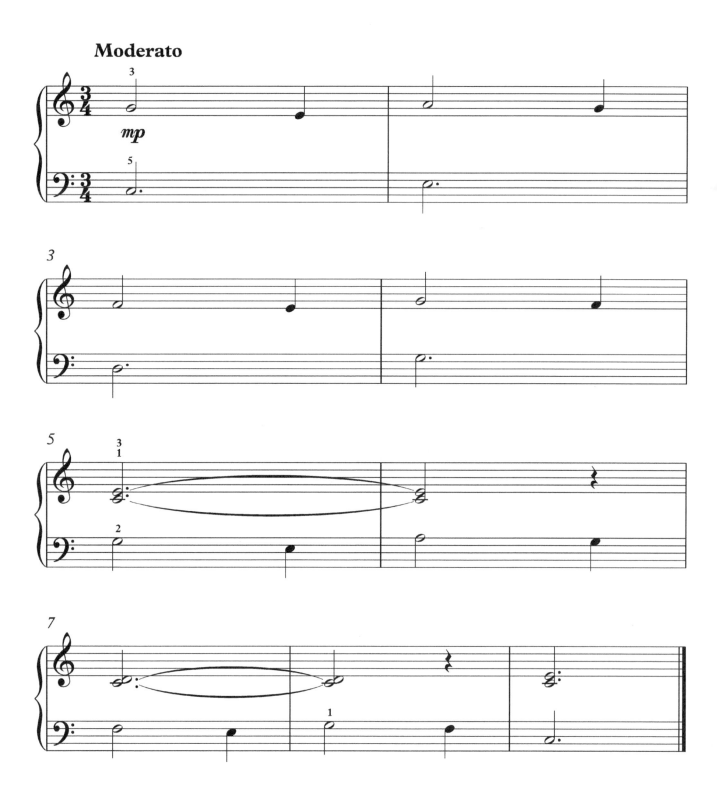

Symphony No. 9, Mvt. IV (Theme)

Dvořák composed a total of nine symphonies. His last one was finished while residing in Spillville, Iowa, with his family in the summer of 1893. It has earned the name "New World Symphony" and is frequently performed.

Allegro

Silhouettes Op. 8. No. 5

Although famous for his symphonies and concertos, Dvořák also wrote many works for the piano. This charming collection of twelve pieces was composed between 1865 and 1879. Be sure to contrast the dynamics when the melody repeats.

Briskly

String Quintet No. 12, Op. 96 ("American")

In addition to *Symphony No. 9*, Dvořák composed this work while living in Spillville, Iowa. Its nickname is "American." Play the theme brightly and upbeat.

Prague Waltzes B. 99

Prague Waltzes was composed in 1879 at the request of the organizers of the prestigious National Society Ball. They were worried about the state of dance music in Prague and reached out to a number of composers for submissions. Pay attention to the silent measures (3 and 6), and count three full beats.

Romance Op. 11, *from* Mvt. I

This work was published in 1879 and was originally for violin and orchestra. In addition to keeping the melody lyrical, focus on the left hand playing smoothly and melodically.

Moderato

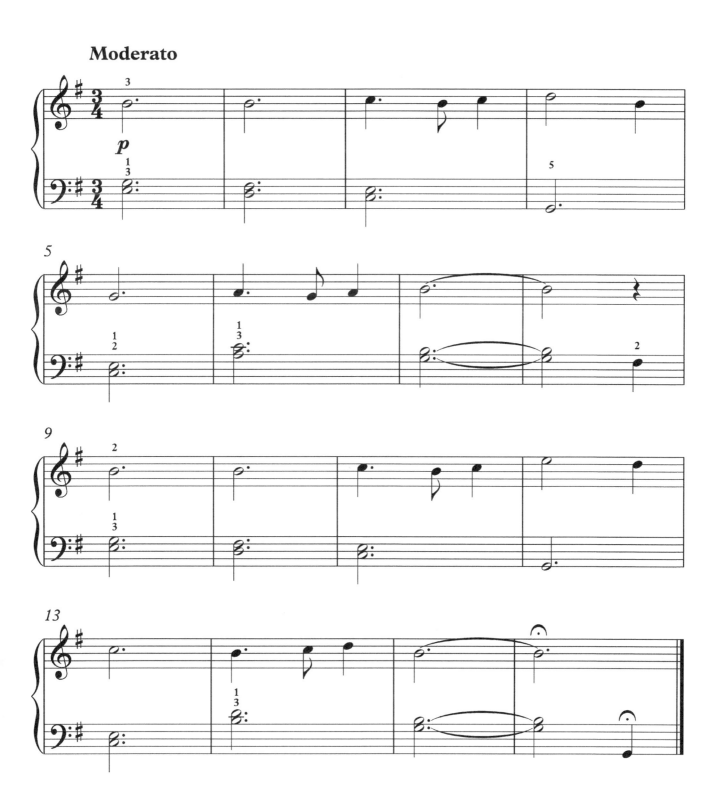

Symphony No. 8, Mvt. IV (Theme)

Symphony No. 8 was composed in 1889 while Dvořák was living in Bohemia. It is more cheerful and lyrical in contrast to his previous symphonies. Pay attention to the triplets in measure 7. The three notes should be played over two beats.

Waltz Op. 54, No. 7

This waltz is the seventh in a collection of eight composed between 1879 and 1880. Following up on the success of *Slavonic Dances*, Dvořák continued to write music for dance halls. Play elegantly and evenly, with both hands moving as one.

Romantic Pieces Op. 75, No. 1

Dvořák composed this cycle of four pieces in 1887 for violin and piano. It was based on sketches of smaller works he wrote to play with his friends. He was a violist and found great enjoyment in arranging and performing smaller works.

Allegro moderato

Symphony No. 9, Mvt. I (Theme)

This moving melody is the opening theme to the first movement of *Symphony No. 9*. The first four measures serve as an introduction and are played softly. When the theme arrives at measure 5, crescendo into a forte and quickly recede back into piano by measure 9.

Song to the Moon *from* Rusalka

Dvořák's most beloved and performed opera is *Rusalka*. It tells the tale of a water nymph (mermaid) who wants nothing more than to become human after falling in love with a prince. In this aria, she asks the moon to reveal her love to the prince.

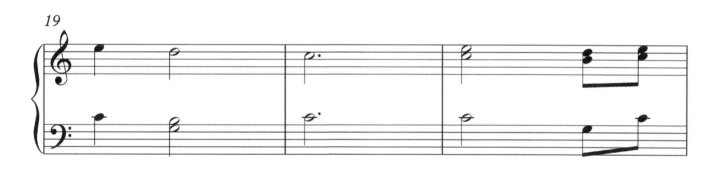

In a Ring! *from* Two Little Pearls B. 156, No. 1

In a Ring! is a toe-tapping work meant to evoke folk dances. The original title, *Do Kola!*, implies a circle (or a ring) dance (the "kola"). Be mindful of the frequent shifts between piano and forte, and use that contrast to help propel the music forward.

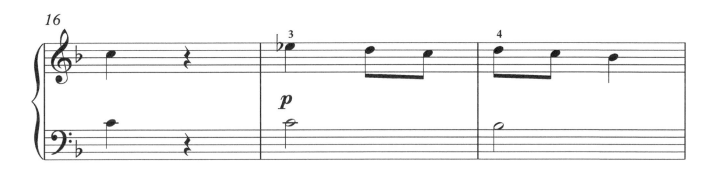

Bacchanale *from* Poetic Tone Pictures
Op. 85, No. 10

In music, a *bacchanale* is a piece depicting revelry and celebration. This one comes from a colorful collection of thirteen works entitled *Poetic Tone Pictures*. Keep the tempo upbeat, adding a bit of revelry.

Songs My Mother Taught Me
from Gypsy Songs Op. 55, No. 4

This popular work comes from a collection entitled *Gypsy Songs*. It is a cycle of seven songs set to poems by Adolf Heyduk. The text tells a melancholy story of passing down songs to children from previous generations, which are not with us anymore.

Mazurka Op. 49, Pt. 2

A *mazurka* is a lively dance in triple meter. This work was originally written for violin and piano and is dedicated to the virtuoso and composer Pablo Sarasate. Keep the tempo moving, and emphasize the downbeats.

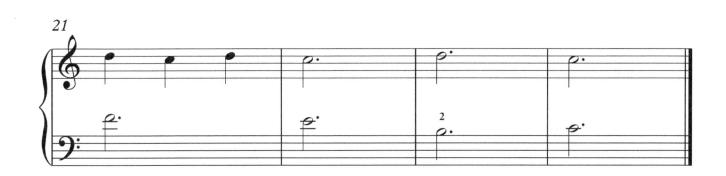

Cypresses B. 11, No. 2

At the age of twenty-four, Dvořák fell in love with an actress named Josefina Cermáková and composed a cycle of love songs entitled *Cypresses* for her. Although the love was unrequited, there was a twist: Josefina eventually became the composer's sister-in-law.

Cello Concerto Op. 104, Mvt. I

This majestic concerto offers many opportunities to develop expressive techniques. In the opening, project the power of the forte. In measure 7, create a noticeable contrast with the plaintive piano. And be sure to bring out the left hand as the ending returns to forte.

Allegro moderato

Grandpa Dances with Grandma
from Two Little Pearls B. 156, No. 2

The second work in *Two Little Pearls*, this charming dance offers some challenges. Warm up with A minor and C major arpeggios. Most of the melody is based around these two arpeggios, with other notes added in between.

Allegretto

Mazurka Op. 49, Pt. 1

This opening theme sets a moving and upbeat mood. Play the melody crisply, keeping your fingers firm and without lagging on the keys. And before playing, look over the accidentals (sharps and naturals) in measures 13–15.

Allegro moderato

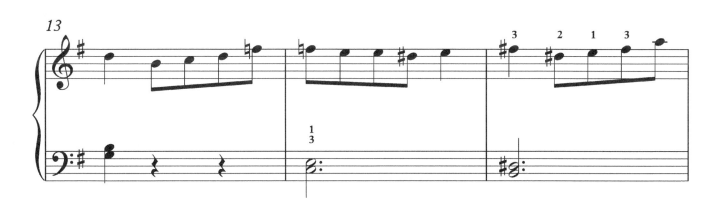

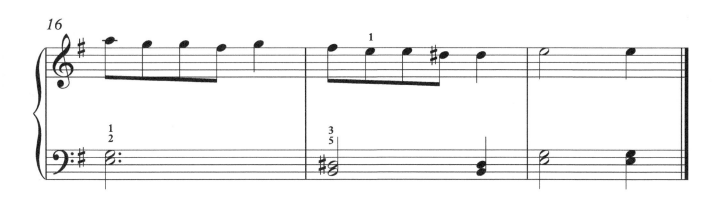

Stabat Mater Op. 58, No. 6

"The Stabat Mater" ("The Mother Was Standing") is a hymn depicting the Crucifixion through the eyes of Mary. In this movement, the choir sings, *"Fac me vere tecum flere"* ("Make me truly weep"). The musical texture here is a chorale, where each note represents a voice in a choir.

The Question B. 128

This piece was written in 1882 but not published until after Dvořák's death. It has an abstract quality to it, created by the accidentals (sharps and naturals) beginning in measure 4. Play expressively, bearing in mind that this is a musical "question."

Allegretto

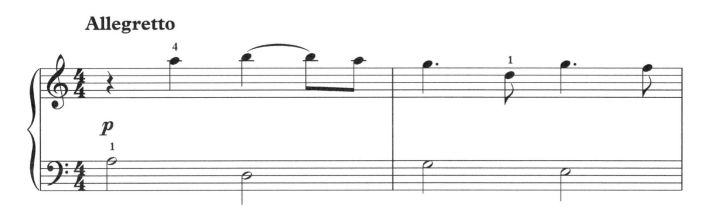

Chorus of the Water Nymphs *from* Rusalka

In the beginning of the opera *Rusalka*, three water nymphs (mermaids) appear and sing to the Water Gnome, ruler of the lake. Notice that there are three notes (voices) throughout. These correspond with the three nymphs and should sound as one.

Capriccio B. 188

A *capriccio* is an upbeat, lively, and playful musical composition. Dvořák projects just such a mood in this piece. Keep the right hand light and moving, with the left hand providing a steady pulse.

The Water Goblin Op. 107 (Theme)

"The Water Goblin" is a tone poem (a composition inspired by a theme or work of art). The story is based on Czech author Karel Jaromír Erben's poem of the same name. Play forcefully and evenly.

Ballade Op. 15

The tempo marking here is *lento*, which means "at a slow pace." Keep the notes even, and be especially mindful not to rush the sixteenth notes and triplet.

Serenade for Strings Op. 22

This elegant work remains one of Dvořák's most performed pieces. Play with a regal tone, using the sixteenth notes to add to the melody's charm.

Dumka Op. 35

A *dumka* is a Slavic musical form with contrasting sections. The term translates into "a thought" and denotes music of an introspective nature. Play descriptively and perhaps with some introspection of your own.

The Noon Witch Op. 108 (Theme)

Just like "The Water Goblin," this work is a tone poem inspired by the writings of Karel Jaromír Erben. Dating back to Slavic mythology, the Noon Witch would appear at the stroke of noon and take away misbehaving children.

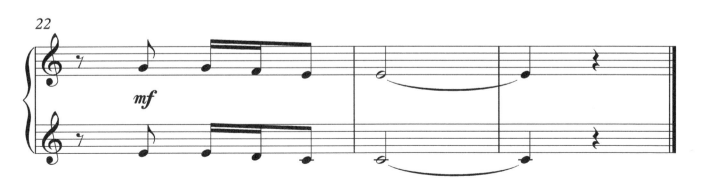

Symphony No. 9 ("From the New World"), Mvt. II—Largo

Perhaps Dvořák's most recognizable melody, it is also known as the song "Goin' Home." The symphony was completed during the composer's three-year visit to the United States. There is a museum in Spillville, Iowa, in the apartment where he lived and finished this symphony.

Serenade for Wind Instruments
Op. 44, Mvt. I

This stately melody opens the first of the four movements of the *Serenade for Wind Instruments*. It was originally written for two oboes, two bassoons, and three French Horns. Perform with the precision of a march, evoking an older time.

March-like

Slavonic Dances Op. 72, No. 2

Dvořák was proud of his Czech and Slavic heritage, finding a huge source of inspiration in it. With this fervor, he set about composing a number of nationally themed works, including two sets of *Slavonic Dances*. In this example, play elegantly and look over the accidentals (sharps and naturals) before practicing.

Violin Concerto Op. 53, Mvt. I

Violin Concerto was composed in 1879 but did not premier until 1883. It has since become a solid part of the violin repertoire. Notice the echoes between the voices. Play them evenly and identically.

Violin Concerto Op. 53, Mvt. II

The second movement of *Violin Concerto* opens with an adagio. Play slowly and expressively. There are a number of different moods in this short excerpt, so be sure to bring them out.

Adagio

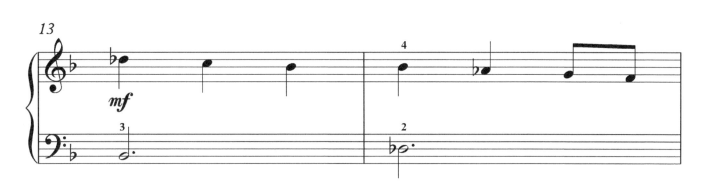

Six Piano Pieces Op. 52, No. 5

In this excerpt from *Six Piano Pieces*, the left hand serves as a timekeeper for the music in the first half. Be sure to practice it separately, and add the melody when ready. The second half presents a contrast in rhythm and dynamics.

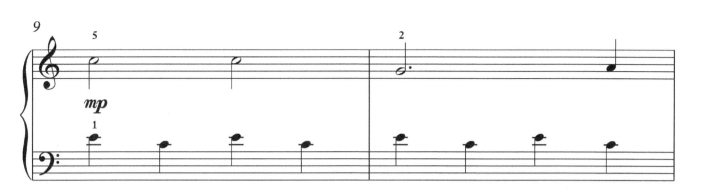

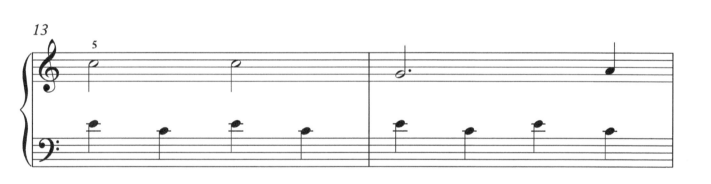

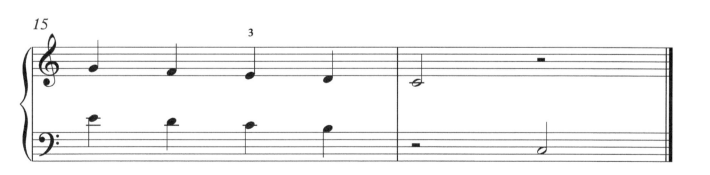

Humoresque Op. 101, No. 7

This famous melody comes from a collection of seven other humoresques for piano. Play with a lively and bouncy feel. Note the fingerings, and move your fingers (and wrists) into place in time for the next note.

Allegro moderato